CW00818766

THE ETERNAL GIFT:
Coping with the grief of losing a beloved animal

By internationally acclaimed animal communicator Lauren McCall

This is the book that demystifies how animals experience their life and death, and helps pet owners understand the love connection that remains after your animal has gone.

DEDICATION

To Dad and Roo. Thank you for showing me the way.

ACKNOWLEDGEMENTS

Neither this book, nor my journey in writing it would be possible without Helen Dunford. "Thank you" doesn't begin to cover it. Your support and inspiration makes it possible for me to "follow my bliss". I am also very grateful to my patient friends who read and re-read this book in draft form and made wonderful suggestions and contributions: Debby Potts and Kathleen Braza. Your input and support were invaluable.

I would also like to acknowledge all of the wonderful animals both living, and on the Other Side, who have contributed directly and indirectly along the way.

All images by Clay Myers
www.claymyersphotography.com

DISCLAIMER
Some of the names of animals and people have been changed to protect their privacy.

© Copyright Lauren McCall 2009 * www.integratedanimal.com

ISBN 978-0-9843142-5-6

AUTHOR BIO

Lauren McCall

Lauren McCall is an internationally known animal communicator, author, and Tellington TTouch Instructor. Her book, *The Eternal Gift*, is based on her popular seminar *Losing a Loved Animal* that helps people deal with the loss of a beloved animal companion. *The Eternal Gift* was a best seller in Japan for 14 months, and was published in Korea in 2012. Her new book, "Let's Talk to Animals" was published in Japan in 2011.

Lauren has also been a featured speaker at seminars and conferences on the topic of life and death from the animal's perspective. She has an international client base for her animal communication work and she teaches in the US, Canada, Europe and Japan. Lauren lives in Oregon, with her partner, a dog, cat, guinea pig and a very sweet rabbit.

For more information about Lauren, and to learn more about how you can communicate with your animal, go to http://www.integratedanimal.com/AC_learning.htm#ac

© Copyright Lauren McCall 2009 * www.integratedanimal.com

Table of Contents

INTRODUCTION 6

CHAPTER 1 7
The Animal's Wheel of Life
"Life within death, death within life"

CHAPTER 2 13
The Dying Process
"There is no perfect time to die."

CHAPTER 3 21
Letting Go and the Nature of Love
"I have happiness and joy. I am free. I am home."

CHAPTER 4 26
Reincarnation
"We've been together before and will be again"

CHAPTER 5 34
The Other Side
"Where I am, there is only unconditional love"

CHAPTER 6 45
The Eternal Essence: A Guiding Light
"I am still with you and always will be."

CHAPTER 7 55
Coping with Grief and Loss
"I understand about death and dying, but it still hurts"

CHAPTER 8 63
Conclusion
*"In this life I achieved the balance between being useful
and a little bit useless. Ah ha, a masterful stroke! What a
most agreeable life. My life has been full of fair currents
and fair winds."*

© Copyright Lauren McCall 2009 * www.integratedanimal.com

INTRODUCTION

What happens when dogs die? Do cats go to heaven? What about rabbits or horses? Most of you reading this book have lost, or will lose, a beloved animal. Your companion has died, passed on, gone over the rainbow bridge, to heaven, or as some of us like to think of it, returned home. They have made that voyage that takes them physically away from us and into a realm that exists outside our daily human consciousness. Just as we ponder what happens to us when we die, so too, we wonder about our animals. Animals for the most part view their passing as a wonderful journey back home to a place filled with unconditional love, joy and perfect bliss. The heavenly mysteries of life, death and reincarnation are concepts that many spend a lifetime trying to grasp. But does it have to be so complicated, so out of reach of our understanding? The animals that I have spoken with don't think so.

With a few notable exceptions, my messengers, teachers, and guides into exploring beyond the confines of human consciousness have been animals. It's not that they have greater insight than the human spirit is capable of, but I do believe that they are closer to, and more comfortable with, the natural cycles of the body, mind and spirit than most humans. Many animals, probably yours included if you were able to talk with them, would probably explain with clarity and simplicity some of the most fundamental questions we ask when faced with death and loss.

When I talk about animal communication, I am talking about communicating through a telepathic connection. Animal communicators can connect telepathically when the animal is physically present; or sometimes use a photo or a description of the animal if the communication is being done at a distance. With telepathy, distance is not an issue and I have no trouble connecting with animals anywhere in this world or the next from my home in Oregon. Every soul, every animal, every person has a unique vibration. When we are connecting to an animal we are tuning into their vibration, just as you would tune your car radio into the frequency of your favorite radio station. Most people talk to their animals all the time; it's just learning how to listen to the reply that stumps most humans.

My work as an animal communicator has enabled me to delve deeper into the interconnectedness of death and life. When I began working with clients and connecting with animals that had died I did so with a sense of trepidation. I was apprehensive about what the animals would tell me about their dying and their death. Would their stories express pain, anxiety or perhaps regret at having shed their mortal fur? And what would I have to report back to their grieving person (or people) who just wanted reassurance that their loved one was happy, free, and not alone in a cold and lonely void?

I am happy to report that the overwhelming feelings that the animals transmit to me are a bursting sensation of joy and love. It's the kind of love that makes your chest

© Copyright Lauren McCall 2009 * www.integratedanimal.com

swell and catches your breath. The kind of feeling that in the end, is so big that it is impossible to describe and can only be felt. I am pleased to say that I now look forward to helping people connect to animals that have transitioned. I look forward with certainty to being able to tell people how wonderfully the animals are doing as well as who they may be with. It is a joy and an honor to carry back messages from the other side that their people will hold as precious gifts. Connecting with animals in that place where souls dwell gives me a rush of the boundless love that they feel on the Other Side.

The death of one of my animal friends is still a great source of sorrow to me, just as it is for you. It is part of the bargain that we enter into when we love beings that almost always die before we do. When one of my animal companions dies I grieve mightily because I miss him. I feel lonely, sometimes lost, and I almost always chide myself for loving so much a treasure that I know I cannot keep forever. As I struggle to come to terms with my loss, understanding that my beloved animals are happy and thriving brings me great comfort. I also know that animals have a sense of purpose in their lives so that when death comes, it is an appropriate closing, a conclusion to a chapter rather than an end to the book. This is because animals believe in the eternal cycle of life, death and rebirth.

When I do a communication with an animal I take word-for-word notes all the way through. Using my notes from actual conversations, the focus of this book will be on the words of the animals themselves. I have selected communications with animals that can empower those who have experienced loss. Their words will impart knowledge of the interconnectedness of life and death, and soothe those loving, grieving souls left behind. Though spiritual in nature, this book is not based on any particular religious belief, but rather the point of view of our animal friends. Remember, the messages contained in this book could just as easily have come from your animal.

© Copyright Lauren McCall 2009 * www.integratedanimal.com

You must always look at the
BIGGER PICTURE
and remember that you are on earth to learn.
When you are finished learning,
you are finished.

CHAPTER 1

The Animal's Wheel of Life
"Life within death, death within life"

Animals are much more comfortable with the rhythms of life, death and reincarnation than most people. Why is that? When I connect telepathically with their 'higher selves,' they seem to be able to recall how the whole process of the eternal cycle works. Onna, a Bernese Mountain Dog I spoke with, said: "It's all a cycle. Life within death, death within life. It's all there to be lived and enjoyed." Before going further, I would like for you to have at least a conceptual understanding of the cosmic wheel of life, death and reincarnation as the animals see it.

In the beginning, at the core of it all, lies the universal cosmic force, the Oneness, the Great Spirit, God. We are all connected to this life force. It is our essence. It is who we are. Ultimately it is what binds us together. Within the universe lie vast worlds, planets, stars and tangible matter including the human and animal physical body. Along with the world that we can see and touch resides the realm of the spirit; those energies, essences, thoughts and feelings that we cannot touch, yet know or sense that they exist. Our souls, and those of our animals, live in this domain. Depending on the culture, this place is referred to as heaven, nirvana, paradise, the Other Side, Elysium, and so on. Animals mostly call it "home." For them, it is that permanent place that we return to each time we die.

I asked for further clarification from Roo, a wonderful Malamute I had the privilege to share my life with until her death at 14. I'll talk more about Roo later, but for now I'd like to share with you a conversation I had with her about the Wheel of Life.

Roo

Lauren: What happens after you die?

Roo: We return home to review our life.

Lauren: To what end?

Roo: To see whether we learned our lessons, and accomplished our work.

Lauren: Can you tell me more about that, what lessons, what work?

© Copyright Lauren McCall 2009 * www.integratedanimal.com

Roo: We choose our species, and in fact our physical bodies, based on what lessons we need to learn in the next life time. So an animal, for example, might choose a body and a life with or without people where they have to learn patience. Perhaps their physical body is impaired and they have to wait for someone to always do things for them. Or perhaps it is their person who is trying and requires them to be patient.

Lauren: I see. Can you give me another example?

Roo: Of course. Let's take you. You were working in an area that was not your life's work. I came into your life and led you back onto the path that you needed to be on. Now you are finally doing your life's work.

Lauren: Yes, I agree and I am grateful to you for that.

Roo: You're welcome. But you see you helped me in that life too, and in others past. It is always of mutual benefit if not in one lifetime, than in another. Always, there is balance. That's the way the universe is. Balance. Good and bad, stronger and weaker, smarter and well, stupid.

Lauren: So you choose the body in which your soul will reside knowing roughly what your life will entail?

Roo: Roughly, yes. That is what enables us to choose the right body for our lessons. If we had no idea what the life would be like, we would have no way of picking a situation that would suit our learning.

Lauren: And how many times does this happen, the life, death and reincarnation cycle?

Roo: Hundreds. Life is non-ending because life is not limited to the physical bodies you have on earth. There is much more to it.

Lauren: Animals mostly seem to know this; they seem to be more comfortable leaving their earthly bodies.

Roo: Yes. We are one with the earth. The earth is one with the universe. Outside of the learning station of earth, there is love and bliss and harmony. We know it is there and are always happy to return to it. In doing so we return to ourselves, to the Oneness that is all of us.

Lauren: Thank you, Roo.

Roo: You're welcome.

This return to Oneness that Roo described is probably why most of the animals I talk with willingly accept their death, or the death of those close to them. The exceptions I have seen to this have arisen with the sudden death of young animals that sometimes

© Copyright Lauren McCall 2009 * www.integratedanimal.com

were taken by surprise. That is not to say that all animals that die young are surprised by their death. Here is a conversation I had with a kitten who died at about seven weeks. Many, many people, including myself, loved this kitten and tried very hard to save her.

Below Lady Jane makes reference to reincarnation which we will explore further in Chapter 3.

Lady Jane

Lauren: We are so sorry this happened. Clare and Pete are very upset- they loved you very much.

Lady Jane: Yes, I know they tried everything, it wasn't meant to be.

Lauren: Can you tell us why or what happened?

Lady Jane: I contracted for a short life. It was my first incarnation on earth. I wanted to be able to get out quickly if I didn't like it.

Lauren: Oh, how unusual. What did you think?

Lady Jane: I will certainly come back and stay next time. There are wonderful caring people out there.

Lauren: Yes there are, but be careful who you choose. I'm glad this was a positive learning experience for you, but it was very hard for many of us.

Lady Jane: I'm sorry it wasn't my intent to hurt anyone. But Pete and Clare can learn that all beings have their path. The purpose isn't always clear, but there is always a plan.

Lauren: Yes, I see. Do you know what you will do next or when you will come back?

Lady Jane: Not yet, but I will return as a kitten, that much I know. Please thank Clare and Pete and everyone else who helped me. I learned a great deal in a short time.

Lauren: Go with love, go in peace, go with light, go with God.

Lady Jane: Thank you. Good-bye.

Lauren: Good-bye.

Lady Jane knew her life would be short. Her death was no surprise to her and she clearly believed that she would come back. The loss of a being to anything other than the fullness of old age is distressing to us all. We feel short changed, cheated on the being's

© Copyright Lauren McCall 2009 * www.integratedanimal.com

behalf and for ourselves. It seems to be contrary to the natural order of things. Lady Jane and others with whom I have spoken teach us that theirs was not a 'meaningless death', nor a 'waste of a life.' How comforting to learn that even the youngest that pass from our care do so with a sense of purpose, dignity and even with a sense of accomplishment.

I would now like to share with you parts of two communications with horses. The first horse, Darsie, had just been euthanised at the age of 22. You will see in the conversation that people came to try and help the collapsed Darsie get back up on her feet and get her moving around. As it turns out, she was too old and too tired to get up, she was ready to go. The second communication is with Angel, another horse, alive at the time, who lived with Darsie for most of her 22 years. As Darsie and Angel were friends of mine, I am communicating with them on behalf of myself, rather than their people. They lived with my friend and business partner, Debby Potts. Unfortunately, Debby and I were teaching at Best Friends Animal Sanctuary in Utah when Debby got the news they had to put Darsie to sleep. I did this communication in a motel room a few hours after Darsie's death.

Darsie

Lauren: Darsie are you there?

Darsie: Yes, wow. This is different. I have been in an earthly body for so long. This feels so light and free.

Lauren: Debby and Harry want you to know how much they love you.

Darsie: I know. I love them too. We had a good life, didn't we?

Lauren: Yes, I'm sure you did. Debby wants you to know that the people there did all they could to help you.

Darsie: Yes, I know, it doesn't matter now. I was afraid they wouldn't get me up, it felt different this time, more tired. I was ready to go.

Lauren: Debby wanted to be there with you, she is so sorry that she wasn't there when you passed.

Darsie: Debby is always with me. She is a light I will carry inside me always- a gift. We were gifts for each other.

Lauren: Is there anything else you would like to say?

Darsie: It's peaceful here- come join me, I'll be waiting!

© Copyright Lauren McCall 2009 * www.integratedanimal.com

Lauren: I will tell them, Darsie. We send you love and light for your journey on.

Darsie: Thank you, I am not afraid.

Remember Darsie's words, "I was ready." "This feels so light and free." "I am not afraid." Now let's hear from her dear friend, Angel.

Angel

Lauren: Angel, this is Lauren.

Angel: Yes.

Lauren: How are you? Do you know what happened to Darsie?

Angel: It was her time. I feel so deeply sad. We have been together as a family for so very long.

Lauren: Darsie is worried about you.

Angel: I'm OK but I will be sad and lonely for a while.

Lauren: You know the people with Darsie before she died were trying to help her.

Angel: I know. They don't understand though. Sometimes you just have to let go. There is a natural order of things that you can't fight and Darsie was so tired. I tried to get her up too. I asked her and asked her even before the people came. But she was finished. We had a chance to talk before she went.

Lauren: That's wonderful that you had that time with your friend.

Angel: So much to say, and nothing to say.

"So much to say and nothing to say." Angel knew and understood, as did Darsie, the gentle inevitability of Darsie's death. There is an acceptance there. No sense of terror. There certainly is a sense of loss at the passing of a lifelong friend. However, I neither sensed nor heard fear for either the one dying or the one left behind. Let's remember Darsie's words: "It's peaceful here. Come join me, I will be waiting." Of course, Darsie was not suggesting that everyone she loved die on the spot. "I'll be waiting," meaning "I'll see you when it's your time to be here; it is a wonderful place to be." Death comes when it comes, and how can it be anything other than perfect when it signals our return home? In the physical world, we see things as good and bad. To the soul there are only lessons.

© Copyright Lauren McCall 2009 * www.integratedanimal.com

My life is almost over. I'm tired.
　　　I want to be with my FRIENDS,
　　　　　　　they are here.
　　　Waiting.

CHAPTER 2

The Dying Process
"There is no perfect time to die."

No matter how much we prepare ourselves for the death of a loved one, are we ever really ready? It's the, "I knew this day would come, I just didn't know it would be today" syndrome. And whereas many people cling to life because they fear what lies beyond, animals, in the vast majority of cases, do not have that fear. Often they are mentally and spiritually prepared for their death long before physical death comes. I have spoken with animals up to a year before they have actually transitioned who were completing things that they wanted to do on earth in preparation for their passing. Perhaps they needed to finish learning a life lesson; or maybe they needed to help their person prepare for the loss. Almost always, they have their eye on the bigger picture, the inevitable transition to the realm of the soul and the journey home. So while it is so very hard for us to let go of someone we love, many people have found comfort in their animals' calm acceptance of their own deaths.

The animals share with me that they, like people, have 'transition teams' waiting to help them move from the physical realm to the Other Side. These are souls, animal and sometimes human, that your friend has known either in this lifetime, or a previous one. In the context of human transitions, many of us are familiar with stories of people who just before they have died literally see their previously deceased spouse, parent or close friend who have "come to take them home." While human transition teams sometimes comprise animals, so too animals have their human friends with them when they pass.

My own experience of this came at the death of my dear Malamute friend, Roo. Roo whom I introduced in Chapter 1, was my father's dog for her first 10 years. They had a very close bond, one that spanned several lifetimes. When my father died suddenly, Roo came into our household as a very welcome addition. She was a wonderful, stunning dog, both physically and spiritually. As she grew older and developed physical problems, I learned Tellington TTouch (a form of bodywork that stimulates new neural pathways and works on a cellular level to release fear and tension in the body) to help her cope with her aging body. When she was diagnosed with cancer, I embarked on the path of learning animal communication so that I could keep track of her physical and emotional needs. Having Roo in my life precipitated a complete career change from the corporate marketing world to that of serving animals and their people. When the time finally came to help Roo leave her ailing body, I invited a close friend of mine, a psychic, to be present. Lynn arrived at my home just before the vet. She told me that my father was present in the room and that he had come to take Roo home. It was one of the most moving experiences in my life to feel my father's presence while he helped his beloved friend make the final journey home. I was devastated by Roo's death. However, I

© Copyright Lauren McCall 2009 * www.integratedanimal.com

managed to find solace in knowing that those two great beings in my life had been reunited. As for Roo, she has become one of my animal communication guides and I call upon her especially when I am connecting with a deceased animal, or trying to help a troubled one still on earth. Her guidance and wisdom are invaluable to me.

When I connect with animals telepathically, I am usually doing so on behalf of a client. That means that the questions within the conversation are, for the most part, my client's questions. I sometimes interject some of my own when seeking elaboration or clarification. It also means that I am usually speaking on behalf of the animal's person and I ask the questions in the first person as though I'm the client speaking directly to the animal. "I want to know how you are feeling," or "I want to know if you're happy," would both be common examples. (This creates a far more intimate ambience for dialogue as opposed to the "Your mom asked me to ask you…" type of approach.) If I know the animal well, or if the animal's person is a friend of mine, I sometimes speak as myself to the animal rather than represent their person. Please also note that it is common for people to refer to themselves as "mom" or "dad" when referring to their animals, and it is just as common for the animals to reciprocate that point of view. In other instances, animals and people might use their first names or nicknames with each other.

This next conversation is with a dog named Jack. I am especially fond of this conversation because Jack talks about so many concepts that are key to understanding the animal's perspective on life, death and reincarnation. Jack's wisdom touches not only on his body shutting down, but also on transition teams, and several new topics we will examine more closely in later chapters. In this conversation, I am speaking on behalf of Jack's mom, Gail.

Jack

Lauren: Tell me what it's like where you are now.

Jack: It's peaceful. It's warm and safe. When I miss you I can create the picture of walking with you. That's nice. We both miss that, don't we?

Lauren: Yes, I do miss that. Do you have friends where you are?

Jack: I have many. Um, friends, also soul mates, people and animals. I can be alone if I choose or I can be with others very easily. One is never lonely here. There is work to do but it is always interesting and a pleasure.

Lauren: What kind of work is there?

Jack: Well, I am looking at my life as Jack and reviewing what happened, how it went and what more I need to learn.

© Copyright Lauren McCall 2009 * www.integratedanimal.com

Lauren: Did you learn what you needed to? If so, what was it?

Jack: I learned about being faithful. German Shepherds are famous for that and I needed to learn that.

Lauren: That's wonderful. What lessons did you help me with?

Jack: You are at an interesting place in your development [as a soul]. You are moving to a higher level. Much of what I can teach you, you can now learn from my death. Focus always on the bigger picture, the soul purpose. That means that life and death must be viewed in a different perspective.

Lauren: How so?

Jack: Focus on the soul. I am very much alive. Our paths will cross again. This grief is all in your physical body and you are grieving for a body that no longer exists. Leave all that and rejoice in the essence of being [meaning the soul essence].

Lauren: Thank you. That is very helpful. You seem very wise. Have you been human before?

Jack: Yes, once. It's more complicated, harder than being an animal!

Lauren: Yes, I'm sure it is! How many times have you lived on the earth?

Jack: Oh, over 100 I'm sure.

Lauren: When will you come back?

Jack: I have no immediate plans for that.

Lauren: Did we know each other in another lifetime?

Jack: Yes, we have traveled together a few times. Last time was many years ago. I was a cat, white with long hair. You were a woman. We grew old together and enjoyed sharing our lives.

Lauren: How wonderful. I wish you were here to continue to share this life.

Jack: Well I guess I am in a spiritual way.

Lauren: Yes, there is that. I need to talk a little about your death. I feel some guilt about maybe keeping you alive too long. You were crying the last couple of days. Did you suffer?

© Copyright Lauren McCall 2009 * www.integratedanimal.com

Jack: My body was having a difficult time with the shutting down of [body] functions. I felt no pain. [He means he felt no pain because he was spiritually out of his body a lot preparing to leave it behind.] It was also important that you feel that you did everything you could before letting me go. Now you worry that you waited too long? No. This is not correct. There is no perfect time to die. When other beings are involved in your life it becomes even more complex.

Lauren: Why?

Jack: Well, in this case there was my timing and yours, and Dad's. All of those things came together in the best way they could. It isn't always smooth. It was fine.

Lauren: Why did you cry out?

Jack: I expect it was my body closing down and letting go. Animals sometimes cry or make noise to ground themselves.

Lauren: I see. Did you know I was with you when you passed?

Jack: Of course.

Lauren: I always did my best to care for you.

Jack: You did a wonderful job. I am very grateful. I really am.

Lauren: Do you know what caused your seizures?

Jack: My body shutting down. [Parts of his body shut down suddenly rather than gradually.]

Lauren: So I guess you were ready to pass on then.

Jack: Oh yes.

Lauren: Who was on your transition team?

Jack: A black cat, people I have been with before, an orange cat, a bird and another dog. There were many. You are never alone here.

Lauren: That's nice. I'm happy about that. I'm just a little curious about your life before we met.

Jack: Ah. Well, I guess you could say that I was on my path to find you. I lived with street people who were kind but this was not the life I was destined for. I ran away by getting loose from the string that held me.

© Copyright Lauren McCall 2009 * www.integratedanimal.com

Lauren: I am so glad you did!

Jack: Me too.

Lauren: Is there anything you want to say?

Jack: I am touched that I have made such a place in your heart. It is such a gift. Please now move on to that place of light and love. It feels much better to be there. I am a being of light now. For me there is only peace and love. Please share that with me.

Lauren: Yes, yes I will. Thank you very much. I love you and I always will.

Jack: Of course. That love never changes.

Lauren: Good-bye for now then.

Jack: Yes, until we meet, or speak again. Good-bye.

There are a couple of key concepts in Jack's communication that I would like to talk about in more detail. The first is that it takes the body time to shut down. Sometimes the body wears out before the spirit is ready to go, but usually it is the other way around. Often the animal is emotionally and spiritually ready to move on but the body is still hanging on. Why is this? A couple of reasons I think. As beings living on this planet, humans and animals have keen survival instincts. If you are swimming and dive under the water to have a look around, your body lets you know when it needs air. You then swim to the surface as fast as you can. This is an instinctive physiological response, it is not your brain thinking "Gee, I guess I had better gulp some air now, let's swim to the surface." It takes time to shut various components of the body down. Whether death comes as a result of old age, illness or injury, parts of the body are still working and are programmed to keep going as long as they can.

Some of you may have noticed that your animal friend has a sudden burst of energy a day or two before they start to decline quickly. This is something that I have personally experienced with a number of animals and have always found this phenomenon a bit confusing. I would think that the animal was recovering or stabilizing, only to be disappointed. One of my clients, Erin, had a dog named Schooner. My conversation with Schooner finally provided me with an explanation for this sudden "burst of life." We come into this conversation part way through and I am speaking on Erin's behalf.

Schooner

Lauren: Did my making an appointment for your operation have anything to do with the timing of your death?

Schooner: Yes and no. The time of my death was very near anyway. It is not always an exact thing when you die [in other words, there is no set day or time]. So I finished what I needed to do and then left.

Lauren: But you seemed so well and playful before you crashed.

Schooner: This is not uncommon to have a burst of life. It's like a cellular memory in the body. They are fun, but not sustainable.

Lauren: So the idea of the operation helped you move on?

Schooner: I needed to show you that I couldn't sustain that [burst of life]. It wasn't real. I just wanted to experience physical joy one last time.

Jake was a very spiritually evolved Golden Retriever aged about 14. His family asked me to come and talk with him about where he was in his transition process, and to find out if there was anything he wanted or needed. I was speaking to Jake on behalf of his family and I'll pick the conversation up part way through:

Jake

Jake: I have no pain other than the pain you get with old age.

Lauren: So you say you are tired, tell me more.

Jake: It takes ages to shut down the body. People don't realize what a process death can be.

Lauren: Yes, it's true. Are you spiritually ready to leave your body?

Jake: I'm very close.

Lauren: When will you be ready and how will we know?

Jake: By stopping eating I am shutting things down. I wish it weren't so slow.

Lauren: So you are spiritually ready and you are waiting for your body?

Jake: Well, that and I had a few things to finish. And I was waiting for all of you to be ready.

Lauren: We want you to know that we love you very much and we want you to go when it's your time.

Jake: Thank you. That helps. I have been worried about leaving you. I know you are sad and worried about me.

Lauren: Yes. Of course we are. But we are also accepting of the natural cycle of things, of beginnings and endings.

Jake: Yes, that's good. That helps. I feel frustrated that I can't move around and smell things the way I used to. I can sense things, feel the sun on my face, feel the breeze whisper against my fur. But the gleeful, perhaps youthful joy of life isn't there.

Jake's family had also noticed that he seemed to have a vacant look quite a lot. It's like looking into someone's eyes and no one is home. This is not uncommon for animals who are in pain. They are able to spiritually leave their body and stay near by going in and out as they need to. Many of you who have lived with an older animal or person may have sensed when they were fully present with you or not. It is a good thing to be able to leave your body for periods rather than suffer physical discomfort. Jack referred to this when he said he felt no pain even though his body was experiencing seizures as it shut down. Jake was also taking advantage of the opportunity to 'check out' now and again.

A little later in my conversation with Jake I talked with him about the possibility of euthanasia. His family wanted him to go on his own, but they didn't want him to suffer and asked me to check in with him. He agreed that if he began to suffer he wanted help to die, but he wanted to make sure his family was ready to let go first.

© Copyright Lauren McCall 2009 * www.integratedanimal.com

I don't know what else to say
besides I LOVE you.

CHAPTER 3

Letting Go and the Nature of Love
"I have happiness and joy. I am free. I am home."

Physically and emotionally letting go of someone we love is one of the hardest things we ever have to do. I am so thankful that the time to let Roo go was very clear. Not only could I see that she was suffering physically, I was able to communicate with her and confirm that she wanted to go. Unfortunately, it isn't always clear. How many of you have worried about whether or not the time had come to make that final call to the vet? I have. Did I hang on too long? Did I end it too soon? At these agonizing times, animal communication can help a great deal. I have received specific information from animals about whether or not they were ready to go, and some even have expressed preferences about where they wanted to die (usually at home) and who they wanted present at their passing. Some even have views on how they want their remains or ashes laid to rest.

Whether you use animal communication to assist you in your decision making or not, it is very important to tell your animal friends that it's okay for them to go when they are ready. You can tell them yourself; they understand you. The tricky part is that you have to get yourself to a place where you mean it; they'll know if you don't. It is not uncommon for an animal to hang on waiting for their people to be ready to let them go. Let's look at a conversation I had on behalf of a client named Karen. Her dog friend, Kiki, was failing and Karen wanted more insight into where Kiki was in her process of letting go. We'll pick this conversation up part way through:

Kiki

Lauren: Where are you in your transition process?

Kiki: As you know, I am quite close. But it's OK. It's hard to accept this change for both of us on the physical level. But I will always be the light that you carry within you.

Lauren: Yes. And I will always be with you.

Kiki: Yes, that is so.

Lauren: Are you in pain?

Kiki: Not so much. I am a little tired.

Lauren: How will I know when you are ready to go? I want you to know that I am OK with your going when you are ready.

© Copyright Lauren McCall 2009 * www.integratedanimal.com

Kiki: Thank you. That is important to know. I will begin to let go and you will see life drain out of me. I will be listless and the light will go from my eyes. Already I am spending time outside my body.

Lauren: Yes, I can feel that. That will ease your transition process.

Kiki: Yes. And there are those on the Other Side waiting for me [Kiki's transition team].

Lauren: Of course. We have a choice of releasing you at the vet's office, or here at home, which do you prefer?

Kiki: Oh, home, of course. I would like Mama here [Karen's mother] and you can ask anyone else you need to support you. I want it to be peaceful and surrounded by love.

Kiki expressed how important it was for her to hear that her mom was ready to let her go when the time came. She also reminded us about spending time out of the body, about transition teams, and given an option, she made a choice about where she wanted to pass, and what she wanted that to be like. What a wonderful gift when we can offer our beloved animals options about where they want to spend their final moments, and with whom. Of course, this is not always possible for us to arrange. When our own cat, Gordon, was sick with lymphoma we had planned to have our vet come to the house when we could no longer manage his pain. As it turned out, Gordon began vomiting one morning and was clearly in distress so I rushed him to the vet. It was time to let him go. My partner was unable to get to the clinic fast enough to be there at the end and his final moments were not the peaceful transition we had hoped for. I was very unhappy about this and felt badly for Gordon. I brought this up with him a week or so after he passed. Gordon said, "It didn't matter. I could feel you were both there with me and I wasn't really in my body much anyway. Release was sweet."

Release does feel sweet. I first experienced the feeling of release from the physical body during the course of a near death experience. I was sound asleep in my college dorm room when I had what I now understand to be a severe asthma attack. Never having had one before, I was unsure what to do when my lungs started to constrict and my sinuses filled up so that I could hardly breathe. All I could think to do was to get to the communal showers at the end of the hall and get some steam into my lungs. I made it to the showers with some difficulty and remember turning on the hot water tap. After that I must have passed out. What I remember next is floating above myself, looking down on my body with the pure hot water washing over it. Though I was confused, I felt somehow comfortable with where I was, and happy. I felt completely serene and light. Somehow I understood that I had the option to leave my body behind at that time and move on to the Other Side. Though sorely tempted, I couldn't shake the feeling that I had not completed what it was that I needed to accomplish in this lifetime. I clearly remember expressing my desire to return to my body. At that point, I somehow went back into myself, stood up (yes, dripping wet), turned off the water, changed my pajamas and went back to bed. Not only had I suffered no ill effects from the hot water, my lungs and sinuses had cleared up. It was as though I had no residual physical signs of the attack that I believe had literally killed me. In the years since, I have suffered a few more of those attacks and even with the benefit of an inhaler to ease the constriction in my lungs; it always takes at least an hour for my lungs and sinuses to return to normal. I will never forget the feeling I had floating over my body and feeling such release, lightness and joy.

Euthanasia is a difficult option for some people. This may be due to their religious convictions, their notion that it is contrary to the natural order of things, or they are just emotionally unable to end their friend's life. We would all like to pass naturally, preferably in our sleep. Unfortunately for those who may be suffering physically, natural death and its "sweet release" don't always come on demand. When directed by a client to ask the animal's preferences surrounding their death including euthanasia, I show the animal a little movie about euthanasia I have stored in my head. It takes them through the physical process of having their leg shaved, the catheter inserted and so forth. I finish the movie with the feeling of freedom and joy that the animals have shared with me, and that I have felt in my near death experience. I think it's important for the animals to understand the process of euthanasia and the finality of it. Then they, and their people, can make an informed choice. In my experience, the vast majority of animals choose not to suffer in their bodies and opt for release.

For those of you who have agonized and felt guilty that you let go too late, or too early, I'd like to share a communication I did for Kathy and her deceased cat, Mickie. Kathy was in the process of starting a new relationship; she felt unstable and felt she needed Mickie as an anchor. She tried very hard to keep Mickie with her on the earth. She just couldn't let go. After Mickie finally passed, Kathy grew worried that Mickie had suffered at being kept in her body too long. Kathy felt guilty and it made her anxious about repeating her 'mistake' with the animals she currently lived with. I am speaking on Kathy's behalf.

Mickie

Lauren: I'm sorry for not letting you go sooner, causing you to suffer.

Mickie: You know there is nothing to feel guilty about. You were changing your life and it was meant to be. Look at how wonderful your life is now. Your life with Chris is fulfilling so many of the things you wanted and filling the loneliness that I could not fill.

Lauren: I am so sorry that I prolonged your life longer than I should have.

Mickie: A valuable lesson about letting go and the nature of love. Love is unchanging and everlasting. It knows no time, no boundaries and has nothing to do with the bodies we inhabit. You must learn this lesson and let go of the rest. I have happiness and joy. I am free. I am home.

© Copyright Lauren McCall 2009 * www.integratedanimal.com

Lauren: Are you planning to come back?

Mickie: Yes, sometime, but not for a while. I am still learning from my life with you. You are still learning I see. It's good for both of us. Look for balance. Life, death, illness, health, happiness, sadness, they are all the same thing- part of life. You must accept them all and move on.

Lauren: Can you forgive me for any pain I caused you?

Mickie: There is nothing to forgive. It was my path at that time to help you with yours.

Lauren: Thank you, Mickie. I love you and miss you.

Mickie: I know. You can talk to me, I hear you.

Lauren: Thank you so much.

Mickie: Be at peace. I am.

Mickie clearly did not see any reason for Kathy to feel guilty. She felt it was her path to help Kathy through that difficult time. Let's remember Jack's words from the previous chapter when his person expressed regret at having kept him alive too long:

"It was also important that you feel that you did everything you could before letting me go. Now you worry that you waited too long? No. This is not correct. There is no perfect time to die. When other beings are involved in your life it becomes even more complex."

The nature of love is to transcend things like imperfect timing.

Though we have walked the earthly path together,
our JOURNEY TOGETHER is not done.

We will meet again.

CHAPTER 4

Reincarnation
"We've been together before and will be again"

What is reincarnation? Simply put, it is the rebirth of a soul (or being) into a new body. It is about returning to a body on earth to continue to learn lessons for the purpose of spiritual evolution. Reincarnation is embraced by some religions and rejected by others. On this subject, as in many others, animals take a spiritual, not religious view. In fact, it has been my experience that animals do not adhere to anyone one religion. It's not as though cats are Methodist, dogs are Jewish or llamas are Buddhist. They seem to have a more eclectic approach, and animals tell me that they do believe in reincarnation. We have already touched on the subject of reincarnation during the course of my conversation with Roo in Chapter 1. Now I'd like to look at this fascinating topic in more detail and explore some of its ramifications.

There is a wonderful proverb attributed to the Australian Aboriginal tradition that I would like to include here. While this is not a direct quote from an animal, most people would agree that the Aborigines are very in tune with the earth and animals. I think this summarizes the animal's point of view very well:

"We are all visitors to this time, this place. We are all just passing through. Our purpose here is to observe, to learn, to grow, to love...and then we return home."

In the theory of reincarnation, souls choose to experience lifetimes that often involve associating with other soul beings (animal or human) that you have known on the Other Side to assist each other on your respective paths. Like many people, you may personally have had the feeling that you already know a person or an animal that you have just met. In all likelihood, you have met before, either on the Other Side, or in another lifetime.

A conversation with a dog named Bushwacker relates the wonderful past-life connection he has had with his person, Cheri. At the start of the conversation Bushwacker is talking to me directly; we were friends and had spoken before. As the conversation moves on, I begin interjecting Cheri's questions and speak on her behalf.

Bushwacker

Lauren: Hi Bushwacker.

Bushwacker: Hello, I've been waiting for you.

© Copyright Lauren McCall 2009 * www.integratedanimal.com

Lauren: Why?

Bushwacker: I want mom to know how wonderful I feel and how happy I am. And also you must tell her that I am nearby when she needs me. And she may need me in the near future.

Lauren: I'll make sure she knows that. That's wonderful. She wanted me to tell you that you are forever in their hearts and their minds.

Bushwacker: Yes, I know. I can feel that very clearly. I think they are getting used to my being gone.

Lauren: Well, it takes time for us humans especially when we love so deeply.

Bushwacker: Of course, it is the same for us. The bonds of love are not limited by the difference in our species. Nor by the dimensions of space and time. Where I am now, love is boundless.

Lauren: How wonderful. Were you a person or a pet in my past life? Who were you?

Bushwacker: I was an elephant that worked with you in the jungles. Like Bushwacker, I was steadfast and loyal. We worked as a team and lived a long and happy life together.

Lauren: How fabulous. Are you coming back? Will you be with me?

Bushwacker: I do not know yet. I am sure we will travel (together) again, I just don't know when.

Lauren: Very well. Is there anything you would like to tell me?

Bushwacker: I am not far away. Near enough to help you and Dad. Just call on me. You may ask me questions and I will answer. You will feel my answers in your heart and know they are true. [By 'true' I think he meant that Cheri would know it was really him talking to her.]

Lauren: Thank you so much. Our connection continues to be a blessing in my life.

Bushwacker: Mine too. Love and be loved.

Lauren: I will. Good-bye.

Bushwacker: Farewell.

You may remember the conversation with Jack in Chapter 2, where he recalled that he was a cat in a past life with his person, and that they "grew old together." Animals are often able to recall one or two past lifetimes they have had with their person.

© Copyright Lauren McCall 2009 * www.integratedanimal.com

How does the process of choosing a body for a being's next lifetime happen? And does this mean that our deceased animal will return to us in our lifetimes, just in a different body? What the animals have taught me is that when on the Other Side, the previous lifetime is reviewed by the animals and their "spirit guides" or "mentors." In this process, they evaluate how successful or not they were in this lifetime in accomplishing their objectives and learning their spiritual lessons. Animals, like people, travel in "soul groups." It is thought by many that this is the true meaning of the familiar expression "soul mate." In fact in this context, soul mates are beings that you have traveled with in past lives or have spent time with on the Other Side.

It is common for people in a particular soul group to travel with animals in a particular soul group. The groups often overlap or mesh like cogs rotating and interconnecting. I rather like this rotating and interconnecting circular image as it recalls the Animal's Wheel of Life we learned about in Chapter 1. People and animals as represented by the teeth on the wheel travel their own cycle, but come together and interconnect at various points.

When the animal is ready to return (the amount of time varies widely but the average seems to be two to three years) they choose a body and a life that enables them to work with other human and animal beings. These interactions are for their own benefit, and for that of the other souls. Or, in the case of the kitten we met in Chapter 1, Lady Jane, in order to see what it's like to live on earth for the very first time.

For many of us who have lost animals this reincarnation scenario seems to offer the possibility that our beloved animals could return to us, just in a different body.

Technically, this is possible and it certainly does happen. Unfortunately, the animals tell me that it does not happen as often as we would wish for ourselves. Working on the premise that beings reincarnate to learn lessons and to evolve, it does make sense that they would go to new people and new homes to experience new lifestyles, patterns, teachings and ways of interacting with new people and animals. However, I have certainly connected with living animals who tell me that they have been with their current human companion before, perhaps in the person's childhood or even in the more recent past. It just doesn't appear to happen as often as people might think.

I have had many people ask me to check if their new animal friend is a reincarnation of another specific animal who died in their lifetime. They tell me that this animal feels comfortable, familiar, and may even have some of the behavioral or physical characteristics of a previous animal. More often than not, it *is* an animal that the person has met before, but it is often an animal that has been with them in the person's previous lifetime(s). It is the reunion of soul mates that has created that feeling of familiarity.

Another question that people ask me is whether or not animals can incarnate into human bodies. This is a difficult topic for some people because they may feel that humans are inherently superior to animals, more evolved. I believe that humans are not

© Copyright Lauren McCall 2009 * www.integratedanimal.com

"better" than animals, just different. I asked for clarification on this subject from our beloved Bernese Mountain Dog, Byron. Byron died while I was writing this book at the age of five years nine months after losing his battle with cancer. I knew that he wanted to help me complete this book, so I asked him some specific questions on this topic:

Byron

Lauren: Byron, I want to know if animals can take human form when they reincarnate. Many people believe that humans and animals are too different for this to happen and that we just evolve on separate paths.

Byron: We are all part of the whole, the Oneness. We are created out of the same fundamental cosmic energy, just in different forms. We all evolve and change, though for some it takes more time than others! In the sense that evolution is moving forward, or at least changing, we are all on paths going in the same direction.

Lauren: My understanding is that we are all made up of this energy and thus have a certain vibration, or frequency that speeds up as we develop. [Science and especially the field of quantum physics tells us that everything is energy, it just vibrates at different rates making the energy more or less solid.] What does that have to do with incarnating as an animal or a human being?

Byron: Animals, and mammals especially, have a basic physiological structure that is very close to humans. We all have organs, lungs, a heart and so on. But the human body is a little bit more complex. In truth the lives of humans are more complex than that of most animals. It isn't as though we have simple lives or that we don't have our own hopes and dreams and complex thoughts, but it is different.

Lauren: How so?

Byron: Humans deal with their personal lives, work lives, paying bills, organizing their social lives, those of their children, and so on. There are many, many levels of human activity and you all seem to do them all at once. This is complicated and needs a certain evolutionary level to achieve it.

Lauren: So are you saying that a being requires a certain vibrational level to be able to handle a human body?

Byron: Yes.

Lauren: So animals can become humans if they achieve a certain level of [vibrational] development. Does it happen often?

Byron: Not so often and many animals who try it don't like it. Being human I'm sure has its advantages, but it isn't easy.

© Copyright Lauren McCall 2009 * www.integratedanimal.com

Lauren: No, it isn't in many ways. Have you been a human?

Byron: No. I'm not sure I want to be. I can still learn a lot from choosing an animal body.

Lauren: So taking human form is not something that animals aspire to?

Byron: Not at all.

Lauren: Do humans become animals?

Byron: Occasionally to learn something very specific. Like what it feels like to be hunted.

Lauren: Yes, I like that example. Thank you very much for helping me with this complicated subject.

Byron: Sure. It's just not so complicated from where I sit. [He means on the Other Side.]

Learning lessons is something that animals living and deceased often refer to when I connect with them. It is, as I mentioned at the start of this chapter, why we reincarnate. We learn lessons, and we help others learn theirs. Animals are often very clear about what they were (or are) here to learn and what they work to teach their people. This is a part of a conversation with an Australian Border Collie named Turbo. He lived with a friend of mine who is quite an accomplished dog trainer and agility instructor. I'll pick this conversation up part way through:

Turbo

Lauren: I'm not sure we reached our full potential together in some things but I know that you were my best friend and for that I thank you.

Turbo: You were growing and evolving and still are. It was my role to change the path of your life a little. I was a working dog in more ways than one. I was working outside with you and inside with you. [They were working together physically and spiritually.] That was our agreement.

Lauren: I see. Thank you. Is there anything I need to know or learn from our time together?

Turbo: I think you got it all. Just let it go and see our relationship for what it was, a wonderful loving partnership where we learned from each other.

Lauren: What did you learn from me?

Turbo: I learned a lot about people. How different they are, how sometimes difficult they can be. For you, try to relax more and take life as it comes. Be more patient with yourself. If you were already perfect you wouldn't need to be on earth. Me either.

Lauren: That's true. It's hard to maintain the bigger picture sometimes.

Turbo: Yes, it is. Keep doing it though. It's all that matters. Ask yourself "Why is this happening to me in the bigger picture?" Only when you ask that and grasp the much bigger lesson and purpose will you be able to move on.

Lauren: I do try.

Turbo: It's not about trying. It's about allowing.

Lauren: Right. Thank you.

Turbo: Helping others is what I do best!

Lauren: You are a master at it.

Turbo: [He smiled and giggled.] Thanks. See you then.

Lauren: Up there or down here?

Turbo: In your heart. I'm always there.

Lauren: Perfect. And you'll find me in yours.

My friend Raelene and her buddy Turbo had a wonderful working relationship together both on a physical and spiritual level. His advice to Raelene about asking her inner self "Why is this happening to me?" helped to clarify why she incarnated in this life, and what she was supposed to learn from a particular situation. Turbo helped Raelene to gain some perspective even after his death.

Some lessons take a lifetime to learn, but those lifetimes are not always long ones. Are the lessons any less valuable because a young life was cut short? Can we judge the quality of a life based on how many months or years on the planet? This next communication was with Emmy, a severely handicapped kitten I spoke with when she was just 5 weeks old. Emmy was Lady Jane's sister (from Chapter 1). She died a week or so after we spoke.

© Copyright Lauren McCall 2009 * www.integratedanimal.com

Emmy

Lauren: Hi Emmy.

Emmy: Hi.

Lauren: You are a very special cat.

Emmy: Yes, I know!

Lauren: I'm wondering what your purpose is here in this lifetime.

Emmy: Try, try, try. In my last life I was lazy, lazy, lazy.

Lauren: You have chosen a difficult body.

Emmy: Yes, it may be a very short life but I will get the feeling of trying my best, being my best. I need to know what this feels like in my soul and in a body.

Lauren: It is a very good lesson, but a hard one.

Emmy: Just because a lesson is short, doesn't mean that it isn't worthwhile.

Lauren: Yes, you are so right. Is there anything that we can do for you?

Emmy: No, I will follow my path so long as I can. It's enough.

Lauren: Thank you Emmy. Go with light, go with love, go with God and may your journey be a fruitful one.

Emmy: Thank you.

What I love about this conversation is that we learn that there is always something to be gained, lessons to be learned. With a touch of humor, Emmy teaches us that life is neither wasted, nor meaningless, no matter how short or how difficult. This applies to animals in shelters too. They too have their path and should be honored for the beautiful beings that they are; I think this is much more helpful to them than just pitying them. Although we all wish for a day when there are no more homeless companion animals waiting in shelters, we cannot judge or decide the nature of their current path on the planet. Perhaps they are waiting for a special person who needs them. Maybe it's you. Maybe the animal waiting for you is an old friend, a soul mate.

The love we had TRANSCENDS space,
time and even species.

CHAPTER 5

The Other Side
"Where I am, there is only unconditional love"

The thought that when we die we are going "home" is one that has been brought up at various points in this book. Animals feel that physical life is a joy, and it is meant to be enjoyed. They (and we) can do things when they are in a body that often can't be done or experienced in the same way on the Other Side. Eating, having your head scratched, feeling your hooves strike the ground as you gallop across the pasture, or being groomed by your best friend are all examples of things that are felt more strongly and are best savored in the physical body. And of course when our animals die, it is very much their physical presence that we miss. With all of the knowledge and understanding I have about the Other Side and how wonderful it is, I still grieve deeply when my companions die. It's natural. We are here in the body, and bodies like and become attached to other bodies. The physical presence of another is something we find familiar and comforting, and it is how we interact with beings on the most basic level. When animals die, that corporal part of them dies, and our interaction with that physical being is gone.

However, death does not have to be the end of our connection with that being on a spiritual level. We can continue to interact but in a different way, as exemplified in the many conversations in this book. Many of you have felt the presence of a deceased loved one. When I connect with an animal on the Other Side, I am blessed to be able to feel the cosmic unconditional love that they report experiencing, and it is joyous! What follows is what some of animals have shared with me about what the Other Side is like and about what it "physically" feels like for them to be there. In general, animals tell me that it feels less complicated when they leave their earthly bodies.

A Bernese Mountain Dog named Onna lived with a TTouch friend of mine. After Onna's death, Lynne asked me to connect with her. She wanted to know if Onna had met up with a couple of their dog friends who had preceded Onna to the Other Side:

Onna

Lauren: We were wondering if your friends Panzer or Jyha were there waiting for you?

Onna: Yes, and other animal souls I had been with before. You are never alone here. It is a much easier place to be than earth.

© Copyright Lauren McCall 2009 * www.integratedanimal.com

A Dutch cat named Jewel lived with some friends of mine, Carmen and Benno. I spoke with Jewel on their behalf sometime after she died. The vast majority of animals I connect with show themselves to me in their previous form, in other words, they look like they did in their last earth body. This is mainly so that we can recognize them and so that I know I have connected with the right being. This is useful when I am communicating with an animal I didn't know, though it isn't essential. Jewel has chosen to show me her soul, her energy form, and it sparkles like a jewel!

Jewel

Lauren: Hello, Jewel. I can see why they named you that. You are very beautiful.

Jewel: Thank you. My true form is very beautiful, so many colors!

Lauren: Yes, I can see that. Benno and Carmen want to talk to you and they have asked me to help. Is that OK?

Jewel: Wonderful.

Lauren: Thank you. First, how are you doing?

Jewel: I am wonderful. I have finished looking at my life as Jewel and then I begin to look ahead at what is next.

Lauren: Are you pleased with what you achieved with your life as Jewel?

Jewel: Yes, it was a good life. I learned much.

Lauren: Like what?

Jewel: Patience, the joy of giving and receiving. How to share earthly love with different species. That was very special. I learned that love is love, no matter the body or species you choose. It is wonderful and warm in all its forms.

Lauren: Does this feel different from the love you experience on the Other Side?

Jewel: Different yes. More limited. Here the love is unlimited. We are all connected as beings but here we can really feel that connection. It makes the love stronger, bigger.

The understanding that Jewel gave me was that although we can feel love very strongly in our physical bodies (so much so that love's presence or absence hurts sometimes), it is even more intense without the body. It is almost as though the body acts as a filter of sorts. Perhaps the feeling of cosmic unconditional love is just too powerful for us to handle through our physical senses. When writing the Introduction to this book,

© Copyright Lauren McCall 2009 * www.integratedanimal.com

I found it a challenge to describe how this unearthly love feels as I felt it during my own out-of-body experience. What can I say? It's beyond words.

Let's now learn how individual animals feel "physically" on the Other Side. We first met Angel the horse in Chapter 1, just after her friend Darsie had died. I spoke with Angel again just after her death. Since we were old friends, I am speaking to her on my own behalf. When I called to Angel, she came to me looking much younger!

Angel

Lauren: Hello Angel. Where are you now?

Angel: I'm still nearby but on my way.

Lauren: How do you feel?

Angel: Oh, wonderful! I can hear and see clearly, my feet just fly, I can run and jump and my spirit is soaring.

Lauren: How wonderful. We are all very shocked. Did you know you were going?

Angel: I started to feel a little odd in the afternoon. Then I was gone. It was quick.

Lauren: Your mom and dad miss you.

Angel: Yes, I know. But I had a great life, didn't I? Full of fun. It was different when I got older, but still good.

Lauren: I am so glad. Is there anything you want to say to your mom or dad?

Angel: Be happy for me. Try to find happiness, and joy and love where you are. It's all that matters. Try to feel the light. It's wonderful. ['Light' as in the universal cosmic force.]

Lauren: OK Angel, thank you. Enjoy your journey home and feel the love we send you along the way.

Angel: Yes, thank you. I do. And tell mom and dad to be happy.

Lauren: I will. Good-bye for now.

Angel: Good-bye.

It is not unusual for animals who died at an older age to show themselves looking younger, usually middle aged. I am not exactly sure why this is the case, perhaps they feel it was their physical and emotional prime. I love Angel's description of her feet flying and her spirit soaring. Even animals that don't normally fly give me the feeling that they can soar. Shortly after his death, our lop-eared rabbit friend, Ben, came flying around me saying "I forgot how much fun it was to fly!" It was a very amusing picture I can tell you.

The next conversation is with a dog named Kobi. He too has something to say about how it feels to be on the Other Side, but he is also mindful of how his people are grieving for him. I am speaking on behalf of my client. Susan and her husband, Mark, were out of town when Kobi died. Kobi visited Susan in spirit and woke her up from a sound sleep some hours before his physical body actually died.

Kobi

Lauren: Hi Kobi. Oh we miss you so much.

Kobi: Oh, I know, I feel your pain. I wish you could feel the joy and happiness I feel. The total love, the light, the freedom. My only grief at passing is that you and Dad are in pain.

Lauren: Yes, it's very hard. Hard too that we weren't with you when you passed.

Kobi: Oh, I passed much earlier. It takes time to shut down the body but I came to you when I was passing, you know that.

Lauren: You have left a big hole that we simply cannot fill.

Kobi: Odd, since I am much bigger, brighter and stronger now than I ever was. How hard that I cannot share this with those I love.

Lauren: Yes. Will you be near us for a while?

Kobi: Yes, I will be very near for a few days. Then I will be accessible to you in your quiet times and when you call me.

Lauren: Good, thank you. Is there anything else you want to say to us?

Kobi: I love you and always will.

I have always wondered what animals on the Other Side did with their time. I specifically asked this and several other questions to a Greyhound named Azik. Speaking on my own behalf, I found this to be a very illuminating conversation.

Azik

Lauren: Debbie and Kevin love you very much and miss you.

Azik: Thank you. I know. I visit them often. I love them a lot and I am sorry to be apart from them. Tell them I am running free.

Lauren: Yes, I will. I'm sure they will be happy to hear that. Azik, I am writing about the Other Side. What it feels like to be there, and what you do all day. Can you help with those two things?

Azik: Well, it's wonderful to be here.

Lauren: Do you miss your body?

Azik: I miss the healthy body, not the sick one. There is nothing quite like earth though. It is rich and lush and full of wonderful experiences.

Lauren: Do you miss those?

Azik: In a way. Of course it is truly wonderful here too. There is a return to 'Wholeness' here. It is where we come from and where we return to. It's our origin.

Lauren: You mean it is where our spirit, our souls come from?

Azik: That's right. Come from, go back to.

Lauren: So I expect that you are meeting up with old friends, human and animal?

Azik: Yes, that is true. It's fun, really fun.

Lauren: What do animal souls do all day?

Azik: Well it depends on what their job is. I mean, well, first you come back after earth, then we all rest and recover, especially if we had a hard physical life. Like if we were sick. We re-gather our energy.

Lauren: I see, and then?

Azik: Well, like I said, it depends on our job. But the next step is to review our life with a Guide or Mentor. Then you study about what you didn't learn [therefore might need to focus on in another lifetime]; some souls help others out as Guides or Mentors.

Lauren: Tell me about what you study and how you study.

© Copyright Lauren McCall 2009 * www.integratedanimal.com

Azik: We return to our soul groups [beings tend to travel and study together in groups], we tend to all be at about the same level. We talk about where we all are in our evolution and where we want to be. We talk about what went right and what went wrong in our past lives. Like maybe you need to repeat a lesson.

Lauren: Can you give me an example?

Azik: Well, you have been learning patience for more than one lifetime!

Lauren: That's very true. What else do you study?

Azik: We look at the earth and other places and try to decide how we as souls and as embodied souls [when they reincarnate] can help the animals, people and the planet.

Lauren: Help with respect to what?

Azik: Where to begin? There is so much that is out of balance.

Lauren: So you work with your energy?

Azik: Yes, sometimes even as a species collective.

Lauren: Can you give me an example of how that works?

Azik: Horses. Horses are working to try and reconnect people and the earth. Either people must exploit the earth because they are poor and suffering, or because they are rich and don't care. That's greed.

Lauren: Yes. It's a big problem.

Azik: Harmony. It's all about harmony. Even poor people need to be in harmony with the earth and the animals. Burning forests and killing the animal's places is not in harmony.

Lauren: I see. Thank you. That is very helpful. May I ask, what is the difference between a Guide and a Mentor on the Other Side?

Azik: Oh, hard to explain. I guess, let's see, well, I guess a Guide is like a Mentor but in the bigger picture. A Mentor might help and advise with one aspect of your life. The Guide might be an overall helper.

Lauren: I think I see. I will try and think of an earthly equivalent to clarify this for people.

Azik: Yes, good. That's hard for me to do.

Lauren: You have really helped, thank you so much. I send you love and light.

Azik: Thank you. And send my love to Debbie and Kevin.

Lauren: I will. I promise.

This next conversation is with a cat named Max. He died at about one year of age, and had been lovingly cared for by a woman, who runs a small cat shelter in Hong Kong. Max had been a sickly cat most of his life; in fact many of his littermates perished before him. We come into this conversation part way through, and I am speaking on my client's behalf.

Max

Lauren: Why did you die so young?

Max: It was interesting to choose a body where I learned so much in such a short life.

Lauren: Oh, what did you learn?

Max: I learned that life is something that you must fight and struggle for sometimes. It is a gift to be valued. I did not have this appreciation before. It was always easy for me, this time not so.

Lauren: So you chose to have a short life this time?

Max: Yes, I am sorry that you and the others suffer and grieve for me. But be glad that I learned such a valuable understanding. In my next lifetime, I will value it [physical life] more.

Lauren: Thank you for that perspective, it helps. What are you doing with your time on the Other Side?

Max: Actually I visit other sick cats on earth and comfort them. For those that have a chance to live, I tell them it is wonderful here [on the Other Side], but that it is worth fighting for their earth life.

Lauren: How wonderful. Have you helped any cats to find the courage to fight for their life?

Max: Yes, three. I haven't actually been with too many cats.

Lauren: I understand. Are the cats you worked with all in Hong Kong where you were from?

Max: Yes. It is a place where I am comfortable.

In Chapter 4 you met Byron, my beloved companion. After his death, I asked Byron what he was up to on the Other Side and he shared some fascinating information with me about choosing a particular species to incarnate into.

Byron

Lauren: What can you tell me about daily life on the Other Side?

Byron: Well, it is purposeful; we don't just sit on clouds all day! [I think I may have had that picture in my mind when I asked the question!]

Lauren: I see. So what do you do?

Byron: We work on our energy [soul energy]. We look at the nature of different species.

Lauren: Why do that?

Byron: So that when we choose another body we can go into a species that suits our needs. Animal species are very different from each other.

Lauren: So why, for example, would you be a dog?

Byron: Dogs that live with people are learning about interspecies living, harmony. We learn about the mixing or interaction of our energies. Lots of other animals are more into their own lives [apart from people]. Dogs go out into the world of people a lot.

Lauren: Yes, that's true. We ask our dog companions to mix in our society quite a bit. What else do you do during the day?

Byron: We learn about oneness, the whole, the creation, the source.

Lauren: Do you mean you look at understanding it?

Byron: Yes, and our place relative to it.

Lauren: What is the ultimate objective?

Byron: Truly being in harmony, being one.

Lauren: Do you have recreational time?

© Copyright Lauren McCall 2009 * www.integratedanimal.com

Byron: Sure. We play. Usually the same species play. Dogs like to play ball, we run. Souls who often like to be birds have flying races and they chase each other.

Lauren: So I assume then that you take on characteristics of a "physical" body to give you species-specific characteristics?

Byron: Yes, sometimes to do specific things like that.

Lauren: It sounds like fun.

Byron: It is!

If you remember, in the conversation I had with Kobi he said, "Oh, I know and feel your pain." Our animal friends who have died do understand and acknowledge our loss. It isn't at all surprising that these loving and compassionate beings are concerned about us even after they die. I would like to share with you one of my all-time favorite communications. It's with a wise and wonderful dog named Huggy who lived to be quite a ripe old age.

Huggy

Lauren: Hi Huggy, it's Lauren again. I'm here with your mom.

Huggy: Yes, that's a good thing.

Lauren: Why is that?

Huggy: She needs and wants to talk about me. It makes her feel closer to me and relieves some of the pressure of sadness.

Lauren: Yes, she is sad. She has some questions for you, is that OK?

Huggy: Of course, I'm not going anywhere [smile].

Lauren: Cute! How are you?

Huggy: I'm wonderful of course. How could I not be? Oh to be free and happy and released. It's perfect bliss and perfect love [where Huggy is].

Lauren: How wonderful for you.

Huggy: Yes, thank you.

Lauren: What have you been doing?

Huggy: Well, I am with Mom sometimes. There are times when it is harder for her than others.

Lauren: Yes. Like when?

Huggy: Nighttime. Times we used to share. Little times when she turns to see how I am doing and I'm not there. Times she no longer has to worry about me.

Lauren: It's hard and lonely being left behind.

Huggy: Yes. Life is a bittersweet experience. What a gift that we had the relationship that we had. It isn't always that way. But it is a connection to draw strength from, to rejoice in. To keep locked away in that special place in your heart. To think of me and smile with joy. For this is what my life was, joy. I could ask no more.

So even though Huggy is in that place where "It's perfect bliss and perfect love," she goes back to spend time with her Mom to try and ease her pain. Huggy's message is a simple one. She reminds us that the connection we have with our animals remains in our hearts, and theirs, even on the Other Side.

The CONNECTION of love is all that remains
after the body dies.
Call to me with love from your heart.
Call in as I soar.
I will hear you.

CHAPTER 6

The Eternal Essence: A Guiding Light
"I am still with you and always will be."

What exactly am I connecting with when I communicate with animals after they have died? What is the part of that being that remains 'alive' even after death? Animals tell me that it is the spirit, the soul, the very essence of the being that remains. When a loved one dies, human or animal, most of us cling tightly to our memories of them; what they looked like, smelled like, their funny and endearing habits, the way they felt when we touched them. Most of these memories are stored somewhere in our mind where we can call upon them when we need the comfort that they offer. But recalling these memories of our loved ones is more than just the intellectual process of storing random memories in our brains. It's about discerning the very core of the being, adding the feelings of love that you have for them, and making those thoughts and feelings a part of who you are. I call these much deeper types of memories, "soul memories." These precious "soul memories" lodged deep within your inner being, will enable you to remain close to your loved one long after your mental memories have faded.

In addition to retaining a connection with our beloved animals through memories, animals that have crossed over can also remain close by becoming a Guide or Mentor to us. You may remember that Azik mentioned Guides and Mentors in the previous chapter. Before exploring how animals can work with us as Guides, let's learn more about the eternal essence, that part of the animal that becomes the Guide. A dog named Boomer beautifully describes how important it is to focus on who the animal is inside.

He teaches us that we should develop a connection with the spirit, the eternal essence, rather than maintaining our attachment to the body.

Boomer

Lauren: Do you have some information or perspective that you would like to share about your death?

Boomer: Humans hold tightly to the body, even after it is gone. They try to hold onto the body of the being as though it will keep them close. This is false. What remains of us is the spirit. This has always been who I am, who I am still. It is my true essence and being. The body is for learning only. To experience the joys and sorrows that one learns upon the earth. It is no more and no less. But then we leave it [the body] behind. You also must learn to leave it behind and seek out the essence that the true being really is.

© Copyright Lauren McCall 2009 * www.integratedanimal.com

This essence that Boomer referred to, along with your emotional memories and mental pictures, is what you take inside of you to create your soul memories. I wanted to get a clearer understanding of what an animal means by "eternal essence," so I connected with my Malamute Guide and friend, Roo. Roo has had many, many lifetimes and is a very wise being. I asked her a series of questions about souls and the essence of beings:

Roo

Lauren: What is the eternal essence and what does it mean to you?

Roo: It is that seed within from which all things grow. It is that piece of us that remains forever connected to the Oneness. [There are many ways in which to refer to "Oneness" such as; Spirit, God, the creator, and so on.]

Lauren: So are you saying that this essence is something that fundamentally connects us all?

Roo: Yes, very much so. Despite our differences, we all eat, sleep, take care of our young and dream our dreams.

Lauren: Can you share one of your dreams with me, Roo?

Roo: I dream of a time when people and animals are treated with the respect they deserve. When each being is regarded as an individual with their own rights and feelings; then the earth will be in a good place. This fundamental lack of understanding is not just between people and animals but between species and races. This means that we often disregard each other's needs and wants. When you truly understand someone, then you make choices that can benefit all, not just one. Lack of tolerance and understanding are the main problems.

Lauren: Are people and animals working on this on a soul level?

Roo: Yes, but this is the type of huge understanding that must come in small digestible pieces that can be understood and internalized. It isn't one big lesson; it is thousands of little ones over lifetimes.

Lauren: I see. Thank you. How can understanding the eternal essence, the soul of an animal, help someone who has loved and lost an animal?

Roo: What people need to understand is that we ARE all connected. Whether you know it or not, feel it or not, it *is* there. Learning to make a connection with who a being really is, lights up that pathway between you and helps you feel each other more strongly.

© Copyright Lauren McCall 2009 * www.integratedanimal.com

47

Lauren: How wonderful. I am seeing that pathway you spoke of as a light connection between souls, an illuminated road into the essence of another.

Roo: Yes. In effect it electrifies or charges the connection, it brings it to life in a way.

Lauren: When that connection from one eternal essence to another takes place, what does it feel like?

Roo: Love in its most pure and unconditional form. Most people don't experience unconditional love; but many people who are close to their animal friends do.

Lauren: Are you saying that animal souls have more unconditional love than human souls do?

Roo: No, not at all. Humans are more complex. They are different. They form more judgment and opinions than animals do. Animals tend to accept what comes; however it comes.

Lauren: I see. But both our human and animal souls contain elements of that unconditional love?

Roo: Yes. In fact, it is the very air that we breathe. It surrounds us completely. [Roo is referring to the Other Side as it is for humans and animals.]

Lauren: Thank you, Roo. As always you have been so helpful. I am very grateful.

Roo: It is always a joy to share information with you.

Lauren: I suppose that is why you are a Guide for me.

Roo: That is so!

Lauren: I love you, Roo.

Roo: And I you.

Roo spoke of making that connection, lighting the pathway between beings. There are many ways to do this and even something as simple as an animal sleeping with you at night can take on a wider significance. James was a delightful cat that Ingrid took into her multi-cat household when he was around three years old. He died when he was about four, and they weren't together more than a year or so. But James made a lasting impression on Ingrid's heart, and I can see why. I am speaking on Ingrid's behalf and we are coming in part way through the conversation.

James

Lauren: It meant a great deal to me that you loved me so much. I felt like your sleeping on the bed was a way of taking care of me.

James: Yes. But more than that, it was a way of sharing our connection in a quiet way. It was peaceful and our spirits could mingle while we slept. You see, we got to share this love that has existed between us for a very long time [over several lifetimes].

Lauren: I miss you so much and look forward to seeing you again.

James: It will happen, here or there. We will always have this connection and find a way to help each other through hard times. This is truly how love works. It works through time and space.

I love the way that James talks about their "…spirits mingling while we slept." For many people, it is only in the realm of sleep that they can escape from their chattering minds and allow their inner selves to emerge. For James and Ingrid, sleep provided the portal through which their souls, their spirits, could interact while they were both on earth.

When animals cross over, they sometimes find ways to bestow upon us a gift. Obviously it's not a gift that you would find nestled in wrapping paper and ribbons, instead it is often a unique and wonderful treasure that can help you remain connected their eternal essence. These gifts may be lessons an animal has taught you (or is still teaching you), an experience they wish to share with you, guidance, or the invitation for an exciting adventure. A wonderful owl named Cleo offered her friend Lisa a very special gift. Lisa was a volunteer at a local bird sanctuary and has dedicated many years to helping rehabilitate wild birds. We pick this conversation up near its conclusion and I am speaking on Lisa's behalf.

Cleo

Lauren: I was so blessed to have you in my life. I'll walk the trails alone to honor you. [Lisa is referring to a wooded area adjacent to the sanctuary where the two of them took walks together.] I am sorry that I didn't get one last walk with you.

Cleo: Oh, we can take one last walk together. Walk on the trail and call me. I will come to you. Tell me things and I will tell you things. You are so sweet and so kind. You give your heart so fully to those you love. It is a wonderful thing but it is very hard when you lose a being you love.

Lauren: Yes, that is the price I must pay.

© Copyright Lauren McCall 2009 * www.integratedanimal.com

Cleo: But think of the happiness you bring and the good that you do along the way. You are like a caretaker. We [owls] bring messages about the earth, about nature, about freedom and the joy of life. You are like a caretaker of those messages because you care for us and participate in sending our messages out. I guess you are really like a messenger too.

Lauren: Do you think so? I hope so.

Cleo: When you are on our walk or in a quiet place where you can sit down, call me. Go deep inside yourself and find me. I will take you on a flight like you have never been on before. I will show you the earth from my perspective so that you can fully see and understand what you are helping to protect. [Cleo showed me, through the perspective of her eyes, flying high above the evergreens and rivers, in and among other birds and swooping back down to earth again. It was one of the most exhilarating experiences I have ever had!]

Lauren: Thank you so much, what a precious gift.

Cleo: You too are precious to us [owls]. I will see you soon then.

What a unique and wonderful experience Cleo is offering Lisa; the opportunity to soar with the eternal essence of another being. Once Lisa experiences it, it will stay with her for the rest of her life.

I think one of the most wonderful gifts that animals can give to their people is to become a Guide or Mentor to them. (I think the two terms, Guide and Mentor, are used interchangeably for many people and animals.) Many people are already familiar with the concept of a 'guardian angel.' Guides are not dissimilar in the sense that they are beings looking out for your welfare and are available to help you should you ask. They are often described as helpers or advisors who can give you a unique and (hopefully) unbiased perspective on aspects your life. I feel very blessed that Byron is now "guiding" me on aspects of this book. After Roo's death, she became one of my communication Guides and I call upon her primarily to help me with animals who have crossed over to the Other Side. She facilitates my connection to them and occasionally, on request, advises me on how to handle a particular issue or problem an earthly animal might be having. However, I am told by animals and people who regularly work with Guides that they cannot help you unless you ask them to.

I would like to share with you a conversation I had with a dog who personifies the guardian angel role. Her name is Norma Jean. She died a number of years ago and had what we would consider to be a traumatic death, though she died at a ripe old age. Her person, Kay, runs Cedarhill Animal Sanctuary, a private sanctuary in Mississippi that cares for abandoned, abused, homeless, and neglected exotic and domestic felines. The Sanctuary is blessed to have Norma Jean as their very special guardian angel who is working with Kay to ensure the wellbeing of the sanctuary and its residents. I am speaking on Kay's behalf.

© Copyright Lauren McCall 2009 * www.integratedanimal.com

Norma Jean

Lauren: How are you?

Norma Jean: [Norma Jean knew that Kay had been concerned about the circumstances surrounding her death.] You have got to let this go. It wasn't your fault. It's hard for me to think of what I can say to help you. It was time for me to go and I was so very happy to be with you as long as I was.

Lauren: Oh, it was so hard and traumatic for me.

Norma Jean: I know and I love you so much. But think of me like your little sunbeam, your ray of light. I help you with the animals. I am like a light presence in the area. [Like an angel.]

Lauren: I thought you were here.

Norma Jean: Oh yes. Here outside and inside of you. I moved from being a part of your outside life [in her earth body] to your inside life. I guide you. You mustn't worry. I am in a much better place now and I don't have to worry about my body. I am at peace and I love my job of helping you with your work.

Lauren: That's wonderful. Thank you. How specifically are you helping me?

Norma Jean: I guide you to make choices that are good for the Sanctuary. [Here she showed me a picture of her as a doggie angel with wings, hovering over the area.] When you ask for help deep inside, I answer. I am like an angel for you and Cedarhill.

Lauren: Yes, I can see that. It was just a terrible way to die.

Norma Jean: No, it wasn't. It was quick. It was painless. It was perfect. It allowed me dignity and grace and I didn't have to fight my body.

Lauren: What was your purpose in that lifetime?

Norma Jean: Grace, joy, love. Now I do it from here. This is the best place for me to help you. Trust me. I always knew what was in your heart and you in mine. I speak the truth. Look at me not with sadness in death, but with joy in life and being able to be with you and be able to help you.

Lauren: Yes, I see now. Thank you. I may need to speak to you again.

Norma Jean: I will always be here for you, as I always have been.

© Copyright Lauren McCall 2009 * www.integratedanimal.com

Lauren: I love you.

Norma Jean: Me too. Always.

How wonderful that Kay and Cedarhill have such a strong and loving spirit to guide them. Alison has Mitsi to guide her. Mitsi, a dog, was dying of cancer at the age of four. I talked with her just before she died and we spoke of her impending transition to the Other Side, what that would mean to her, to Alison, and what Alison could learn from her death. Alison is a life coach in Canada and I am speaking on her behalf.

Mitsi

Lauren: I love you so much. I try not to show too much sadness, but of course it's there. Does it upset you?

Mitsi: Of course it does. This is hard. Leaving you is hard.

Lauren: Do you know why you are leaving now?

Mitsi: It's time to go.

Lauren: What was your purpose in this lifetime?

Mitsi: To be a healer, for you. To remind you that love and joy heal wounds.

Lauren: Yes, thank you. But your leaving now is terribly difficult, how can this help me?

Mitsi: It seems cruel, I know. You are to take the lessons I have taught you and apply them after I have gone. You must fully grasp this lesson [that love and joy heal wounds] and share it with the people that you help.

Lauren: So it is for me and for my clients?

Mitsi: Yes.

Later in the conversation, Mitsi reiterated that Alison should take what she learns and apply it to her work. Sam's dog friend, Thor, was another animal who wanted to continue to work with his person, even from the Other Side. Sam was training to be a naturopath and I am speaking for him.

© Copyright Lauren McCall 2009 * www.integratedanimal.com

Thor

Lauren: How are you?

Thor: I'm wonderful. This is such a fabulous, peaceful, loving place to be. You'l! see one day, but not for a while.

Lauren: No. Not for a while. I love and miss you.

Thor: I know. I know this is hard and I'm sorry. It was time for me to go.

Lauren: Why?

Thor: I was ready inside [spiritually and emotionally]. You were ready inside. I can be of more help to you here.

Lauren: Are you helping me as a Guide?

Thor: Yes, I will be. There are great healing energies here. I can be a healing Guide for you.

Lauren: How specifically can I use your guidance?

Thor: Call upon me as you learn to do your work. There is more to good healing than just knowing where to put [acupuncture] needles or what to give people. There is intent; there is the channeling of love, which is the ultimate healing energy. I can guide you in that way. Help you learn. Help you heal others.

Lauren: Thank you. That will be wonderful.

Thor: Yes, we will be together again, just in a different way.

Lauren: I'm so glad. I miss our close connection. But, of course, I still feel you.

Thor: Yes, you do. When you are learning and doing your work and you don't know what to do, call me. I will help you….I know this is hard, but know that my death was not the end. We have a new beginning, you and I. That is very exciting.

Lauren: Yes, it is and I am grateful to have you as a Guide.

Thor: Just remember to use me!

Lauren: I will.

For those of us who are fortunate enough to have Guides and Mentors on the Other Side, we do have to recognize that there are limitations as to how our Guides can

© Copyright Lauren McCall 2009 * www.integratedanimal.com

be there for us. They can help us recognize opportunities ("Say, that sounds/looks like a good idea"), help us feel things through what is commonly called intuition ("That does/doesn't feel right to me"), and give us help through words and pictures to the degree that people are open and accessible to receiving information that way. It is my understanding that Guides cannot directly influence our choices or our life path. They may offer support and suggestions (or hints) but the choice ultimately remains ours to make.

How long do animals act as Guides for us? It depends. It depends on your personal learning curve and whether you continue to need help and guidance. It also depends on whether or not you use your Guides (if you never use them, they won't stay around forever). Of course it also depends on what else your animal friend needs to do on their spiritual journey. Is it time for them to reincarnate and move on with their own learning process? Are there other people or animals who could use their help more? There are many variables involved. I am very thankful that Roo still works with me some four years after her death. I know she won't be there forever. Byron will stay around to help me until I finish this book, then I expect that he will carry on with what he needs to do for himself. Perhaps you can understand the part of me that wants to take my time to finish this book!

I am not looking forward to the day when Roo and Byron no longer play an 'active' role in my life. But I do understand that I, and they, have managed to capture enough of our inner beings, our essences, to have an eternal connection with each other. No matter how many times I reincarnate, my soul memories of Roo, Byron, my father and other departed loved ones will remain with me as an integral part of who I am. Often this soul memory of another being is represented by your love for them, or theirs for you. Love is the simplest, most powerful, and lasting connection that we can have with another being. A dog named Tuffy expresses this beautifully:

"I am in this place of unconditional love. But I have left a little place in each of your hearts that is like this place. It is full of my unconditional love for you."

And thus, the eternal essence lives on.

If you ever feel lonely or sad,
    please open your heart and
        let all of the love light I have given you
           over the years to pour in.
It will fill your sadness with loving light.

CHAPTER 7

Coping with Grief and Loss
"I understand about death and dying, but it still hurts"

When our animals die, coping with the emotions of grief can become a challenge. In addition, the process is often complicated by the fact that grief over a beloved pet is not fully appreciated in most societies. "It was only an animal; you can always get another one," some people say. For most of us, animals are precious members of the family. They offer us an uncomplicated, unconditional love. They accept us for who we are, warts and all. Your dog, cat, horse, rabbit or bird can remind you that each moment of each day is to be savored and enjoyed, gifts that come from their wonderful ability to be in the here and now. These beings are companions, friends, teachers, students, soul mates. Is it any wonder that we would grieve when they die?

We learned in the previous chapter that we can stay connected to our departed loved ones by retaining the essence of their being, and our connection to that essence. Many deceased animals have told me that their essence remains near us for a period of time, most often to offer us comfort. Recall Huggy in chapter 5. She told me that she visited her Mom sometimes, especially at night and those other times of day when they would normally spend time together. When Roo died, I felt her essence on my left side for five days. Not only did I find it comforting, it also reassured me that Roo was happy and joyful. One woman told me that for a week after her cat died, she could feel the cat jump up on the bed at night and curl up to sleep with her. Sometimes, after our animals die, we just have the feeling that we are not alone. Pay attention to those feelings! If you feel or sense your animal friend, stop what you are doing, become quiet and just listen and feel for what comes to you.

But what about those lonely times when we don't hear or feel anything? We just miss them. All those little habits and routines we have developed with that animal are gone, creating "holes" in your day that appear to be devoid of meaning or purpose. Gradually, those holes get filled again with new experiences and we move on, but it takes time and healing grief work.

For many, that grief work begins with the deceased animal's body. Let's look at how our animal companions feel about their earthly body after their death. This is an important issue for many people who wish to honor the animal's remains in some special way. Some people believe that it will help them to feel closer to their departed friend. In fact, it has become increasingly common for human funeral services to also offer animal cremation or caskets as a more formal way of honoring the animal. Where I live, there is even a company that only offers 'pet cremations.' I find honoring the animal's remains very helpful since it gives me a sense of closure. My partner and I have our animal

© Copyright Lauren McCall 2009 * www.integratedanimal.com

friends cremated and, when we are emotionally ready, we honor them by scattering their cremated remains and planting a beautiful flowering plant in the vicinity. I love the image of the plant thriving and blooming, just as I hope that the being I love and have lost is thriving and blossoming as well.

I am often asked to inquire of a departed animal as to what they prefer to have done with their body or remains. One cat told me that she wanted to be placed near where the children played. A dog wanted his cremated remains cast into the moving waters of a favorite river. Many animals have shared that it is not important to them what we do with their remains; they believe that it is a symbolic act mainly for those of us left behind. One horse, named Oash, explained it this way in response to his person's question about whether or not he liked how he had been buried:

"You know, once the spirit leaves the body it's not very important. It's only a shell. I think it is important to treat the body with respect as it can reflect how you honor the spirit and memory of the being. But this [respect] can be shown through intention, not just how the body is handled. I appreciate the effort you made to honor my body."

Mocha, whom we met in the last chapter, explained that, "My body is no longer who I am, but it is symbolic of who I was."

It appears that as long as you treat the animal's remains with love and respect in honor of who they were and what they meant to you, you can choose whatever means you deem appropriate to help you in your healing.

Establishing a connection with those on the Other Side can help to alleviate some of the feelings of grief, loss and even guilt that can accompany the death of a loved one. It won't surprise you to hear that I believe animal communication can be very helpful in this area. Being able to make a direct connection with an animal and talk about things ranging from the profound to the trivial can be very reassuring. One of the hardest parts of loss is dealing with the day-to-day changes in your usual routine. I still wake up in the morning and expect to feel Byron jump up on our bed, and I still feel sad when he does not. It is of comfort to me in these poignant moments to be able to connect with Byron, to talk to him, and just for a few minutes, to re-establish a feeling of normalcy in my heart and my emotions. Talking to him helps to restore a bit of equilibrium in my heart, as does simply making a connection with his spirit, his eternal essence.

There is no perfect time to connect with animals on the Other Side after they have died, though I would propose some rough guidelines based on my experience. It is a good idea to wait at least a few days after their death to give them time to acclimate to their new existence. This means that when you, or an animal communicator, do connect with them, they will be a little more oriented and have some perspective on things. Generally speaking, we can connect with an animal on the Other Side up until the time that they reincarnate into another body. When they reincarnate, they take their spirit, or essence, with them, and become a different earth being with a new name and a new physical consciousness. Basically, this means that if someone calls to an animal using a given

© Copyright Lauren McCall 2009 * www.integratedanimal.com

name by which they were known and they don't respond, we can presume that they are back on earth. Because animals on the Other Side have memories of their past lives, we can connect with an animal long after they have passed, and even experienced one or two intervening lifetimes on earth, if we get the timing right. As a very general rule, the odds of reaching an animal on the Other Side seem to decline somewhat after two or so years. This is a very general rule, and many animals are on the Other Side for much longer before returning to earth.

In addition to making a personal connection with your animal yourself, or through an animal communicator, there are many books on the market designed to assist you in the grief process. There are also personal suggestions for grieving, some of which are outlined below. Kathleen Braza, a dear friend and nationally known Bereavement Counselor, explained to me that the creation of "rituals" can help us remember our beloved friends in healing ways. She has helped me put together some ideas:

- Write a letter to your animal to help the grief flow. After some time, write a letter from your animal *back* to you. The latter is a unique way for the animal to "talk" to you.
- Create a Memory Box for items like the animal's collar, special toy, tags, etc...
- Create a ritual such as planting a tree or rose bush, or making a donation to the Humane Society on the animal's birthday or anniversary of death.
- Create a scrapbook of photographs or a computer slideshow of your digital images.
- Find someone who is willing listen to you reminisce about your loved one without trying to "fix it."
- Create a ritual involving your animal's body or remains that will enable you to say good-bye, and get some sense of closure for the physical part of your relationship.

How we deal with grief and loss is a very personal thing. Don't feel intimidated by those who may not understand the depth of feeling you have for your lost animal companion, don't let them tell you that you need to "get over it now." Grieving is a process, and it will take as long as it takes. The ways of the heart are mysterious and deep, and they will not be rushed by man or beast.

You may feel at some point that you want to get another animal. Some people worry that if they do, their animal who died will feel betrayed or somehow replaced in your heart. On the contrary, many, many animals who have died have asked me to encourage their people to "share their love of animals" with those who need love and care. Far from being jealous of their people "replacing them" with new animal companions, they are happy that other beings can share and benefit from the love their people have to offer. They are especially keen to encourage adoption from shelters, or to take in strays that seem to "happen" across your path. That stray animal may be wandering on its path looking for you. But do understand that it is still important for you to grieve for your animal friend on the Other Side, even though your home and heart may

© Copyright Lauren McCall 2009 * www.integratedanimal.com

be filled with a new love. It is not a matter of replacing your old friend, just sharing your love with a new one.

For those of you who are not (yet) practiced in the skill of animal communication (and I do believe it is a skill, not a gift), you can certainly contact a professional animal communicator to help you. I'll offer some tips on choosing a communicator below. I would also encourage you to consider learning to make the telepathic connection yourself. I spend most of my working time teaching people just like you how to do animal communication, and while it does take time and a lot of practice, I do believe it is something that anyone can learn how to do. There are a number of "How To" books on the market, some better than others. I offer a multimedia learn-at-home system (DVDs and CD ROMs) to help people reach that quiet place inside where they can hear what the animals are saying to them. While many communication instructors teach using meditation techniques, I do not. I think meditation is a wonderful thing, but it is hard for the average person to learn in a busy world where we seem to be pulled in all directions at once. My approach is a "process oriented" one which most people find quicker and easier to learn.

For those of you wanting to find a professional animal communicator, here are a few useful tips:

1. Find someone with whom you feel you can establish a personal connection. Animal communicators come in all shapes, sizes and personalities, just like any other profession. If you are going to be talking about matters of the heart, like death and loss, you will feel far more comfortable working with someone you feel that you can trust and develop a rapport.
2. Choose someone who has had some experience in connecting with animals on the Other Side. It isn't that talking to animals who have crossed over is more difficult, but it is different. It requires the person be more 'grounded,' centered and balanced.
3. Try to get a personal recommendation from someone. Ours is a profession without a code of conduct or formal standard of ethics, and some communicators are better than others. There is nothing like a personal recommendation.
4. Establish the fee structure up front and understand how your communicator works. All communicators I know of will work at a distance using a photograph of your animal, or at least a good description. With telepathy distance is no barrier and you need not worry about finding someone who lives near you. I currently live in Oregon in the United States, but have clients in Japan, Hong Kong, Europe and Canada as well as various parts of the U.S.

Some communicators talk to the animal while you are on the phone with them, others take your questions and do the communication in advance of your telephone appointment time. I fall into the latter category, but either system works well as long as you don't have to pay a lot of long distance phone charges while the communicator is on the phone with your animal.

© Copyright Lauren McCall 2009 * www.integratedanimal.com

I would certainly encourage you to try making a connection with your beloved animal's eternal essence yourself. You may or may not be able to carry out a dialogue until you become more practiced, but you can probably make enough of a connection to feel their presence. I have developed a guided imagery (a variation on meditation) that will help you get to that quiet place inside I call your "heart space." Your heart space is a quiet and neutral place from which you can connect with animals, and humans, on a telepathic level. I call this guided imagery "The Journey to the Heart" and it is available on audio disk from my web site (www.IntegratedAnimal.com). The audio disk is useful as you can just relax and follow the instructions. However, I am reproducing the exercise below for you to try. I suggest that you read it through several times to familiarize yourself with the steps, then relax and try it yourself. Remember, this takes practice. Don't get discouraged if you don't get results right away.

Journey to the Heart

In a quiet room, find a comfortable position lying down or sitting up. Be in a position where your body can be completely relaxed.

Now that you are comfortable, close your eyes. We are going to move our awareness out of our heads and into our hearts.

Picture yourself in your mind. Now see yourself stepping into an elevator and traveling down, out of your head away from all those busy thoughts, down your neck, past your shoulders, into your chest and stopping at your heart.

This is a quiet place; this is your heart space. This is a place where peace and tranquility come to you naturally.

Think about your heart and notice how the beat of your heart feels.

Notice the steady sound that it makes as it beats. Feel the rhythm it makes.

Notice your breathing; the inhale and the exhale. Allow all of your tension to float away as you exhale.

Now put your attention back on your heart and imagine you are breathing through your heart. Inhale through your heart. Exhale through your heart.

Notice how that feels. Notice the peace that comes from being in this, your special place.

As you breathe through your heart, you are breathing life into this place that is yours and yours alone.

© Copyright Lauren McCall 2009 * www.integratedanimal.com

Now let yourself imagine a place that you find beautiful, quiet. It can be by the ocean, or a mountain meadow. Go there now.

See yourself in this place and notice the colors around you.

Notice the sounds.

Notice the smells of this sacred space as you continue to breathe through your heart. Spend some time in your space noticing as much detail as possible as you look around you. Feel that you are really there before going on to the next step.

As you are in your special, sacred, place see an animal coming towards you.
It may be an animal you know now, an animal from your past, or an animal you don't know. It may be a wild animal. Just allow any animal that needs to be with you today to come to you.

See that animal coming toward you, relaxed and happy.

They are next to you, by your side.

Now look at your animal companion and just imagine what they are feeling, being there with you now. Both of you in that place, together, breathing through your hearts.

Feel that closeness with your companion; that bond, that connection. Feel the love there. Just enjoy those feelings of being with each other.

Let those feelings be in your heart space as you continue to breathe there.

In your heart space, notice if your animal companion has something to tell you. It may be nothing, or they may have a message to share with you. If nothing comes to you, then just be happy sharing this special time.

If you like, you can take this opportunity to tell your friend anything you want to share.

When you are ready, say thank you and good-bye to your companion and know that this place is where you can return to anytime you want to make a special connection with an animal, or a person.

Remember how you are breathing through your heart, the rhythm of your lungs as you inhale and exhale. Remember how you feel now in your sacred space.

Now journey back to this room and slowly open your eyes when you are ready.

© Copyright Lauren McCall 2009 * www.integratedanimal.com

I have used this exercise with many people in many lands representing a wide diversity of cultures and languages. With a little practice, the vast majority of people have been able to make some sort of connection with their beloved animal(s) living or dead. I think it's wonderful that people often feel intense joy at establishing a connection of pure love with their animal friend. Many people find the experience a very cathartic one. One woman related that she was finally able to let go of the guilt she had felt for 11 years at the way her animal had died. Her cat reassured her that everything was as it was meant to be, and that there was no need for guilt in their relationship.

There is no way to avoid the pain of loss when your beloved animal friend dies. But there are things you can do to help heal the pain and transform a physically transitory earthly relationship into a more spiritual and eternal one.

© Copyright Lauren McCall 2009 * www.integratedanimal.com

Love is the eternal gift.

CHAPTER 8

Conclusion:
"In this life I achieved the balance between being useful and a little bit useless. Ah ha, a masterful stroke! What a most agreeable life. My life has been full of fair currents and fair winds."

Are animals more astute than people? This book contains so much profound wisdom from animals. How is it that they are able to know so much and to convey complex concepts, like enjoying the here and now, so simply? People sometimes express surprise at how "wise" their animals are when they are with them on earth, or have become when they transition to the Other Side. Even the most rambunctious and unruly animals can sometimes wax poetic via telepathic communication.

Are animals in fact "wiser" than people? I don't think so, though animals on earth do seem to have less spiritual amnesia than people. For some reason, they seem to be better able to incorporate concepts from their higher consciousness (their eternal essence) into their earthly lives. It may be because when they are on the earth, they are more closely connected to the natural cycles of life, death and reincarnation.

The vast majority of animals I have spoken with in this book have been on the Other Side, where they seem to have a kind of "cosmic library card" with access to all sorts of insights. But to keep this in perspective, when on the Other Side, things like reincarnation, the importance of living in the now, the eternal essence, and other complicated subjects are the stuff of "daily life." Beings, human and animal, can describe these seemingly mystical things with clarity because they are living them.

Animals convey to me that earthly life is precious, and it though it holds many hardships for us, it is meant to be savored and enjoyed. The quotation at the start of this chapter is from a cat named Chairman, who lived on a floating home with his people, Joann and Skip. I think this is a wonderful quotation. In his own whimsical way, Chairman has reminded us of the value of balance and enjoyment in our lives. Animals on earth and on the Other Side are good at reminding us that life is not always meant to be busy, fraught and productive. Those rare moments of stillness, and the ability to do things that might be deemed "useless" just because they make us happy or enable us to regroup and become centered and balanced, are very important.

This very lesson was brought home to me recently by our cat, Kadijah. I was in my office frantically preparing for a teaching trip to Holland. Kadijah was across the room draped over the back of a chair, just observing me:

© Copyright Lauren McCall 2009 * www.integratedanimal.com

Kadijah

Lauren: My day isn't going well. I have a million things to do and I am leaving town in three days. I have to go to the bank, the post office, do email, write an article, teach all weekend, buy dog food [and on and on I went].

Kadijah (Gazing absently from me to the window): Yes, but there is a sunbeam coming in through the window. Let's lay down in it.

Lauren (Taken somewhat aback): Oh. [Pause] Um, OK. Let's do that instead. [And so I did.]

It was a small thing, but lying on my floor in a sunbeam with Kadijah reminded me that in between the times of my self-created chaos, there were moments of peace from which I could enjoy and benefit from.

I recognize that for some people reading this book, the very notion of animal communication may be a strange one. I eagerly await the day when science can explain the seemingly inexplicable, and the door to interspecies communication will be flung open. Until then, I would invite even the skeptical reader to test some of the messages that the animals have given us against their own values and beliefs. Is it that the messages themselves are so foreign to us, or is it merely that they have been delivered to us telepathically that makes them so different?

Animals in this book have told us about the Wheel of Life which continues to turn so that death is not the end of life, but merely the beginning. We have learned that most animals readily accept their death and move on to the Other Side without fear. They crossover with their transition team and are reunited with friends, both human and animal, when they reach "home." The animals further counsel us to maintain our connection with them after death through the soul, the eternal essence.

Some or all of these concepts appear within many of the world's religions or are already within the realm of human experience. For example, I have spoken with hospice workers who readily relate stories of people who are transitioning who see or feel the presence of relatives who have predeceased them. These people will tell their nurses that their friends or relatives "have come to take me home." So too, it is with animals.

When people find out what I do for a living, they more often than not have a story to relate to me about the loss of a beloved animal. For many, their grief is still apparent even though some considerable time may have passed since the animal's death. Often, I will try to give them some comfort by sharing an appropriate insight an animal has shared with me. Despite the fact that they may not believe in animal communication, or perhaps are unsure that an afterlife exists, they are almost always ready to be comforted by the possibility that their animal's essence lives on, if only within their own heart. It is human nature to want to connect with a lost loved one. It is a journey that is done through the

© Copyright Lauren McCall 2009 * www.integratedanimal.com

heart, and I rejoice in the knowledge that the words of the animals can help guide people to that inner essence that ultimately connects us all.

My journey in writing this book has been a fascinating one; at times delightful, fun and interesting, and at times stressful, frustrating and sad. However, I am mostly just humbled by the gifts that the animals have enabled me to share with you. It has brought me even closer to my own loved ones on the Other Side, and I am very grateful to Roo and Byron for their love and guidance. Both of them have surrounded me, and this book, with the spirit of eternal love and joy. They, and the other teacher animals who have helped me, will live on through us all. I leave you now with this final quotation from a Japanese dog named Milky:

"Even the most wonderful lives come to an end.
Each beautiful day has a sunset.
It is the way of things.
But my sun will rise again."

The End

© Copyright Lauren McCall 2009 * www.integratedanimal.com

WANT TO KNOW WHAT YOUR ANIMAL IS SAYING TO YOU?

Simple home study courses can teach anyone to communicate with their animals.

Lauren McCall has spent years developing proven tools techniques that will work for anyone. Her programs are designed to help you discover your own innate ability to telepathically communicate with animals.

Learning tools include:

☐ Animal Communication: Making the Connection and
Deepening the Connection: Double DVD Set: $59.95

For more information, and to purchase these home study courses, please visit:
http://www.integratedanimal.com/AC_learning.htm#ac

© Copyright Lauren McCall 2009 * www.integratedanimal.com

ISBN 978-0-9843142-0-1

16368925R00038

Printed in Great Britain
by Amazon